Published by 10-10-10 Publishing

10-10-10 Publishing

1-9225 Leslie Street

Richmond hill, ON

CANADA

ISBN - 9781928155058

Disclaimer

Dedicated to those that seek smartphone and tablet freedom...

Table of Contents:

Chapter 1

Foreword by Raymond Aaron

So you're ready to buy a smartphone or tablet? The entire process can be overwhelming and it's understandable that you want some help. With Apples (Apple), Berries (Blackberry), and Desserts (Android) models on the market, it's nearly impossible to narrow down the options without having intimate knowledge of what's out there – and that's why you need to get this book.

All of the current trends are covered so you know what's available and what you need. Getting connected is easier than ever. Don't think you need a lot of the features that are available? You do and you don't even know it yet!

Don't get scared – there are plenty of lessons to help you through all of the hard decisions that are in front of you.

By the time you are done reading this book, you will be ready to get started. Walking into a phone or computer store will be a cake walk because you will not only know what you want, but you will know what features are a must and why you want all the features that a particular model has to offer. You may even know more than the sales associate.

Do you know what the difference is between a smartphone and a tablet? Do you need both? All of these questions will be answered so you don't end up with buyer's remorse. This means that you can actually save money by grabbing this book before you do anything else.

It doesn't matter how old you are and how up-to-date with trends you are. This is the book that is a must when it comes to buying a smartphone or tablet in today's day and age.

Apple, Blackberry, HTC, Nokia, Samsung, Sony – you name the brand and it's covered within the pages of the book. Forget about letting a sales person talk you into a model that you don't know anything about. The sales person is in "sales" for a reason – to make money. By listening to one of them, you are going to walk out with the model that makes them the most money but may do nothing for your needs.

This book isn't going to tell you how to use the device. It will help you to decide what device you want, however. This is the most important step in the buying process. You can't move on with technology if you don't know what to spend your money on.

If you have been putting off the purchase of a phone, the time has come for you to buy. You can gain the confidence you need to spend the money on a smartphone or tablet once you have finished reading this book. It's a quick read and will help to make the best purchase for YOU.

Raymond Aaron

Chapter 2

Scheduled Update

Here we are in 2014. Will technology ever stop? To be honest, no it won't. Technology is a blessing to some and a curse to others. Some people engage and love technology, but others avoid and hate working with it. It was not designed for you to cringe every time you work on it. It was designed to make life easier. I want to get you to the point where you can make a very quick decision about what will work best for you so that you do not waste money on something you can't even use. Sounds good? Read on.

Almost two thirds of consumers use some form of smartphone or tablet. Teens, adults, business people, parents, teachers and so many other different classes of consumers are embracing smartphones and tablets to enhance their specific field of interest. Our smartphones are used to do tasks we never even thought could be done away from the traditional desktop PC. We stay connected no matter where we go; we are able to "check-in" to show others where we are. We are able to post photos in an instant of what we are doing and share it with the world. We are all connected one way or another. How do you join that space of connectedness?

Let's start at the beginning. What is a smartphone and what makes it so smart? What makes a smartphone "smart" is that it is able to perform various tasks that are usually done on a traditional PC, any time and any place. Above the basic features of making and receiving a call or sending a SMS, a smartphone has a wide variety of extra features normally found on a more powerful device such as a desktop PC. In essence it's a cellular phone combined with features of a computer. So it's not just a phone... it's a smart-phone! Does that answer your question? No? Well look at it this way, you combine a normal telephone with really powerful parts to make it a super phone with very advanced features! Smartphones are starting to put some desktops to shame with their impressive hardware and software that comes installed on the device. You can browse the web, check your emails, take photos, organize your calendar and check the weather. You can set a reminder for things to do, you can video chat with others and get your way around town with a map.

All of the above is great and I encourage everyone to use those tasks to make life easier but there is so much more available to do on a smartphone that you are missing out on. The already mentioned tasks are usually standard on any smartphone today and thus the purpose of this book is also to show you how you can fully utilize the smartphone's full power to make your life even easier and more productive. What if I told you that you are able to make payments with your smartphone? Learn how to cook on your tablet? See where your loved ones are in a couple of seconds? Do your financial planning? Yes, it's all possible on a smartphone or tablet. I will show you how you can get about doing all of the above later in this book. I even included a free bonus mini app guidebook for you to download to get started!1

I want to explain the current state of technology in 2014. We are living in the digital age of information. Want to learn how to do yoga? Go search Google. Want to read the latest news about any topic? Go search Twitter. Want to see what your friends are up to? Go on Facebook. Want to hire a new employee? Go search LinkedIn. Want to access the encyclopedia? Go search Wikipedia. All and any information is available at your fingertips. I will teach you how to get access to everything you want at any time.

Desktop PC's are not making sales for year on year. Wondering why people are not buying PC's anymore? Something big happened in 2010. Apple released the iPad. It changed everything and started a revolution called the "post-PC era". We are living in that era right now and you see it materialize more and more every day. People are dumping their desktops for tablets. So why is the tablet so popular? It is because of its mobility. You might say that a laptop is mobile but how long does your laptop last without being connected to a power source? What risks are there for carrying around your laptop? How heavy is that laptop?

Imagine carrying around your tablet wherever you go. Its super light, the battery lasts for more than a day and you can do most tasks that your laptop does. Sounds great right? That is exactly my point. Tablets are allowing us to move away from our desks and interact with people wherever we want. We can check our emails; we can create and send off an invoice. We can present to a client a presentation no matter where you are without worrying about a

[1] Please visit www.applesberriesdesserts.co.za to access these exclusive content

power source. We can visually show people what we are thinking. What about carrying thousands of books, magazines and newspapers on a tablet, never needing to worry where you actually last used the book or whom you lent it to? How about having access to all your precious photos and being able to show it to anyone instantly? How about being able to do everything I just mentioned without having to worry about a five minute wait for your computer to switch on, without having to ask where the power source is to charge your laptop and above all not needing to worry about carrying this massive device with you all day.

That is the power and sole purpose of a tablet. It makes your life easier without intervening with your current way of doing things. Tablets are the future of mobility and there is a huge focus on this trend within all major technology companies. Soon no consumer will buy a desktop PC. They will always be used in corporate as they are seen as the workhorses but sales reps, parents, personal trainers and teachers are all adopting this new technology to enhance whatever they do every day to achieve their desired outcome.

Where are we going with all of this amazing technology? We are moving towards a 100% end to end connectedness of the user and technology. It will be able to recognize certain moods, emotions, movements and respond accordingly. We are moving towards a term coined, "The internet of things". Don't we already have an internet? Indeed, but soon every single device around us will be connected via the internet. Every single device will be able to send and receive information to act accordingly. Imagine walking to your house door, it opens automatically only to you. It recognized your voice. You walk into your house and the temperatures automatically adjust to your favorite preset. You have a device called Nest, search Google if you don't believe me, that knew you were inside the room and therefore adjusted it to your preference. How about you go to your supermarket and pay using your smartphone. How about you use your smartphone to board your flight without using any physical flight tickets? We are moving towards the ultimate personalization of your needs through technology.

I can write all day about how amazing technology is for us but I want you to be able to say that technology is blessing your life every day. I sincerely hope that you will be able to talk about how this book has changed the way you use your smartphone or tablet. I hope that you are able to teach friends and family about what you have learned in this book. I hope that I will see you at one of my centers for teaching people how to embrace and love technology. We are moving at a very fast pace of technology and I completely understand that.

I, Quinton dedicate my life's purpose to demonstrating to people technological solutions that will enable them to achieve their specific outcomes in the most effective and effortless way possible.

Chapter 3

What is my password?

Technology will always be evolving. There is nothing to be said about that and the sooner we accept it, the sooner we can start to embrace it and not let it get the better of us. Technology should never be a frustration, that is not its purpose and I really am going to stress this point numerous times throughout this book.

I started my journey with technology when I was five years old, which was in 1997. I was in kindergarten and one day there was an announcement that there will be computer classes for those who wish to do it. I immediately wanted to join, as I had never even seen one before but I was out of my skin excited to start working on them. I remember the computer guy, that's what we all called him, coming to the classroom where I watched every move he made, setting up the computer with the screens and keyboard. I really just could not wait to get started.

Guess how many kids signed up? A whole three! I remember this so vividly, as this was one of my top life moments ever. We did not do anything complex, we simply got puzzles to assemble, colour by numbers and of course spelling games. It was all interactive and easy to use, for me anyway. I guess when you are as young as I was at that time, you are curious and hungry for knowledge and therefore nothing is too big to stand in your way to learn that precious information. The best part was when I received my first award ever and it was for Computer Science. Till today when I look at that picture I swell with pride to know that I was the only one in my kindergarten to receive this award! I do not believe that my intelligence played a massive role in this achievement but it was more the excitement that made it all possible. I wanted to learn and I was open to learn about something I have never seen or used before in my life. We all have that excitement and willingness to learn new things but it fades away when we grow older and I feel that we can all become curious again. We can all learn new things that will make us feel more confident to learn even more everyday.

Today we live in a world with more choice than quality. We are bombarded with an array of different colours, prices and features on tablets and smartphones. How is anyone supposed to know what is going to work for them? This leads to us usually asking the sales consultant for assistance and you will rarely find someone that truly cares about your needs and wants for buying a new device, and they will have their own motives as to the suggestion they present to you. We frequently refer to friends, family and co-workers to give us advice about our next major purchase and also major upgrade of what you are using at the moment. Why do we ask others? The answer is usually the same, "I am not an IT person!" or, "I am too old for this computer stuff!" or, "My children know more than I do about these gadgets".

It's an old excuse and I will soon make you more informed about what is best for you later in this book.

There are couple of scenarios I have seen taking place and I will explain all of them now.

The Sales Guy Suggestion

You go to your cellular shop as your contract allows you to get a new device after two years. You are rarely actually approached when you enter the shop so you have to wait around till someone hopefully recognises you and greets you. Not the best greeting but the sales guy did it at least. He asks what you are here for and you tell him you want an upgrade. He smiles (money on his mind!) and takes you to their current offers of the latest and greatest smartphones on the market. He immediately grabs the latest Samsung smartphone and shoves it into your hands. He then starts to ramble on and on about the many 'amazing' features, he dazzles you with the camera and how fast it switches on and off and how long the battery lasts. You are impressed, why? Someone you assume with knowledge of this product just showed you the features. He has an immediate advantage because you think; he is younger and a sales consultant! Surely he must know what's best when it comes to technology, right? Right...

He's convinced you to take the Samsung, you sign up for a two year contract and off you go.

The Family Suggestion

You have been using your Nokia 3310 for years now without fail. You know how to SMS and how to make a call. The battery lasts five days and you can kick the phone on the ground, it is that durable!

One day it drops in the pool and your incredible reliable cellphone is now a dripping wet piece of plastic junk. You need to get a new phone so you ask your son or granddaughter what cellphone you should get next as they are indeed the youngsters and they know best right? Right. They rant and rave about their iPhone, saying that it's the best thing under the sun. If they said it's the best who are you to argue? You set your mind on getting an iPhone because they said so and off you go to your cellular shop to get your new phone.

Once again, the sales team is not the most eager bunch and slip slop approaches you and asks what she can assist you with. You simply state that you need a new phone and your son advised strongly to get the iPhone. They don't object and simply ask which colour you would like, black is the most popular choice and they hand you the phone that is not within your budget but because your son suggested you go ahead without any other advice.

The Co-Worker Suggestion

Your contract is due for an upgrade, you have been using a Blackberry for the past two years and you absolutely love the "free internet" you get every month, which by the way is not free, you still pay R60 per month for this service. You walk around the office and more than 70% of your colleagues are using Blackberry so it's safe to assume that it's the most popular smartphone, right? Right... You ask your co-worker what he thinks about Blackberry, he loves the "free internet". You ask another co-worker and guess what she says, "free internet". So in this situation, everyone is using Blackberry solely because it works out better for them financially. They don't care or know about other brands. They are not interested to see what else there is to offer and generally they are just following the herd with the same choice. Blackberry it is! Off you go, to your cellular store where you immediately request the latest Blackberry. The sales guy cheers you on and you feel great about this choice. These are just three examples of how we make choices in terms of our next purchase. We rely heavily on the opinion of others and never really dig deeper to question why they are recommending what they are. We don't ask them vital questions and simply accept it as truth.

Let's continue with the story. You feel excited because you have a shiny new toy to play with and to show off to friends, family and colleagues. You feel empowered to have joined the smartphone revolution and I encourage this. You get home and charge your new shiny smartphone for sixteen hours. You don't take the plastic off the screen because you can't bear to scratch this new toy. You are about to embark on a two year journey with this new device. You thought you set your alarm on your smartphone for 6:00AM but it never went off, so you overslept and was late for work. You get in the car and want to try out the GPS like the sales guy showed you but it doesn't work as easily as you were shown. You go into a meeting and the phone blares loudly because you didn't know how to switch it to silent. You take a photo but it comes out all blurry. You try to browse the internet but it says there is no internet connection. You made a successful call but that is about it. How on earth could you have spent so much money on this so-called amazing smartphone and it can't do anything you ask it to do? End of the month you get a bill of over R4000 and you almost faint. What went wrong with the three scenarios?

There was no needs analysis done when you were asking advice on your next purchase. The first suggestion came from a sales guy that did not bother to ask what you need the smartphone for and what you intend to do with the smartphone. There was no sales cycle performed to make the best suggestion of a solution that will work for you and only you. The second suggestion came from your children, who loved their experience on the device and innocently advised the same for you, forgetting you had different needs. The third suggestion was purely a solution that worked for specific individuals because of certain factors like financial comfort. Now you are angry, frustrated and confused. You are regretting the choice you made and even resent the person for advising you to take this smartphone. You feel you made a mistake and wish you had your old Nokia 3310 back with your favourite snake game on it. I feel like that too sometimes. Our past experiences form our future perspective of ourselves and other experiences to come. Now that you had a horrible experience with your new Samsung, iPhone or Blackberry you always will think that you are incapable of operating a smartphone. You lose interest and simply use the smartphone for making calls and receiving SMS's.

It makes me sad to see this happen. Technology has been such a blessing to me and I only wish the same for you. The other side of this story is that since you had a bad experience with smartphones you fall back to the mentality that it is not for you and it's only for the youngsters or the computer nerds. We lost our curiosity and lost our willingness to learn.

We then allow our younger generation to surpass us with their superior knowledge of these smartphones and they continue to always know more than you. They have now taken over your iPad and you barely use it because you are scared to use it because you have to ask your eight year old how to operate it. You are embarrassed to ask so you let it go. They are growing up with this device and learn it even more in depth than you. They are the ones that are curious just like I was when I was much younger. They are assuming this is the norm and let me tell you something, tablets will be the norm very very soon. They are becoming literate on how to use this device and therefore when they are older they will never think twice about how to use it. They are the digital natives of our times. Where do you sit in the equation? Are you playing with your child and their educational games every night or is he playing on his own? Are you shedding the old and enjoying the new? No you are not and you want to change that. I want you to be able to do more than your child can with this device. I want you to do your shopping list, plan for a holiday and edit your family photos with your smartphone or tablet.

So how do you keep up? I strongly feel that it is vital to stay up to date with trends and be aware of what is going on in this world by asking questions, reading the right news and just staying curious. I stay in touch with technology trends all the time but not everyone has to read the tech section of websites and magazines but at least here and there read up. I am glad that many are starting to embrace the internet as a viable source for news but as great as the internet is, it is open for anyone to post whatever they like!

My second bonus for purchasing my book is that I will give you a guide of all the most trusted and informative websites in the internet for you to always go to for the latest and greatest news on technology[2]. You can read them once in a while just to stay informed and in touch with current affairs regarding smartphones and tablets.

Did you know that more than half of the top ten stocks are technological companies? You will soon read about what new technology Google is experimenting on. You will read about the monster earnings Apple report. You will read about the old favourite Nokia and what they are doing to get back to the top. You will read about all ten new smartphones Samsung will announce soon and you will read about the underdog Blackberry on what their strategy is on for recovering from near bankruptcy.

[2] Visit www.applesberriesdesserts.co.za to access this content

There is so much going on with the technology world and the sooner you tap into that, the sooner you will be able to talk to friends and family about the latest technology news. Everyone seems to be in a war over smartphones and you can join the madness of personal choice and brand.

I will cover all major brands in this book to show you the advantages and disadvantages of every smartphone and tablet. You can use my book as a simple reference for informative advice for yourself or others that might be in the market of purchasing a new device. You will be able to use my simple guide to make sure that this next purchase won't be another two years of hell. My third massive bonus of this book is that I will give you a short needs analysis based on your request via email[3].

This is a unique offer and I will make sure you make the right decision. I have expert knowledge on the sales cycle and will easily identify which path will be the right one for you.

I again stress this bonus, a free needs analysis done by me personally!

Please visit my website for access to this exclusive bonus: **www.applesberriesdesserts.co.za**

---

[3] Visit www.applesberriesdesserts.co.za to access this content

Chapter 4

Sweet Apples

Apple Inc. Apple is the youngest in the smartphone race yet is often seen as the leader of the pack. We all have used Apple products at some point in our lives and I can bet you can remember it today. Their work is considered the best in the world and it can be fully experienced with many of their successful products including iPad and iPhone.

History of Apple

1976 – Steve Jobs and Steve Wozniak start Apple Inc in a garage building the Apple I which was released that year too.

1977 – Apple II is released. VisiCalc[4] was exclusive on Apple II, this allowed users access to office tools which made it all the more attractive.

1979 – Steve Jobs sees Xerox PARC for first time and buys it from Xerox. PARC is the most important invention to graphical user interfaces as everything moved to this interface when Apple was designing the Apple Lisa.

1980 – Apple III is released to futher compete with IBM and Microsoft. Apple goes public at $22 per share.

---

[4] The first version of Excel spreadsheets

1983 – Apple releases Apple Lisa, the first personal computer with a graphical user interface but was considered a mayor failure becuase of high price and limiting features.

1984 – Apple Macintosh was released and is considered the first true successful product from Apple. The ad for this product is said to be one of the best ads ever made.

1985 – Tension heats up between Steve Jobs and John Scully which lead to Steve's resignation and startup of NeXt the same year.

1989 – Apple takes their first step in mobile with the Macintosh Portable weighing at 7,7KG!

1991 – Powerbook was released as the upgrade to Macintosh Portable. System 7 was also released with mayor graphical improvements.

1994 – Apple looks into failed consumer markets such as digital camera's, portable music player and TV appliances.

1996 – Steve Jobs' succesful NeXt startup is bought by Apple to bring back Steve Jobs as the CEO.

1997 – Microsoft makes significant investment into Apple boosting needed capital. Rebranding the entire face of Apple was Steve Jobs main goal.

1998 – The all-in-one computer is released: The iMac with 800000 sales in first 6 months.

2001 – Mac OS X is released based on NeXt technologies which became the face of desktop products to date. First retail stores are opened as well as the most iconic product release- The iPod.

2003 – Apple iTunes Store is open to the world soon to become the biggest online store of digital media.

2006 – Apple's market cap surpasses Dell's market cap, big achievement for Apple as Dell's CEO predicted that Apple won't last 6 years ago.

2007 – Apple released Apple iPhone, a completely redesign to the traditional smartphone featuring an all-touchscreen interface. No one anticipated the following success.

2009 – Apple App Store is released.

2010 – The rise of tablets, Apple iPad is released again disrupting the tablet market leaving everyone scrambling to mimic the solid design of iPad. iPhone 4 also released with glass and aliminium design made it very sought after.

2011 – Apple's finances look great, greater than the US Government in terms of finance reserves.

Steve Jobs resigns with iPhone 4S release.

Sadly annouced – Steve Jobs dies from pancreatic cancer.

2012 – iPad 3 with Retina Display is released, furthering the roll out of the widly successful Retina Display technolgy in the iPhone 4/4S.

iPhone 5 with larger sized screen is released, public response was overwhelming with the most successful iPhone release to date.

iPad Mini also released to compete against smaller screensize tablets.

2013 – iPad Air, iPad Mini with Retina Display, iPhone 5S and iPhone 5C is released.

Apple is the real underdog story, starting out in a garage and now prides in making the best products in the world. Apple is aiming at the higher income markets with expensive hardware.

iPhone was the first of its kind with its unique approach to physical design and extremely well thought out operating system named iOS. As explained later, no one expected Apple to be this successful with its smartphone as many even went as far to say iPhone is "dead in the water". iPhone is one of the best smartphones to own, many even claiming it indeed is THE best smartphone to have! You will love using the smartphone no matter your experience level. New users might need to take up on some training while experience users will love and welcome this stunning smartphone. I personally use iPhone and I will not easily switch and will explain in depth later why.

iOS

iOS is the soul of the iPhone. Some say it's the worst and some say it's the best operating software. I have used every single operating system there is to date and I will agree this is a marvel of an operating system but there are flaws that need to be mentioned. Apple is now in their 7th version(8th version coming soon!) of iOS and I say it's their best one. Apple came under fire about their lack of innovation for iOS and became very serious about a radical design that took iOS in another direction when it comes to design. Sir John Ive really pulled a rabbit out the hat with iOS 7, as iOS was revamped, scrapping every single design reference from the previous version and starting fresh. iOS 7 focuses mainly on creating the best smartphone experience around, packed with new features and breathing new life into what was considered boring. iOS comes with great apps preinstalled that will ensure that you are able to do various tasks the moment you switch the iPhone on. iOS is speedy and responsive, you rarely wait for anything to happen.

New users might need some form of startup training material to become comfortable but 99% of the time you will only need to be shown once, after this you will be able to do it at home. iOS is a very simple platform and you cannot "break" the software making your iPhone unusable thus again very attractive to those in the market for smartphones. You are able to email, browse the web, purchase music, set reminders, stay in touch and take photos. The home screen is in a grid format so it is easy to find the apps you need.

The App Store gives you access to over one million apps that will suit most, if not all needs. App Store prides itself with exclusive and premium apps that will delight every interest you might have. I discuss apps later in depth so please refer to Chapter 8 for more information.

iTunes is also part of iOS, as this is the biggest online music shop available to you. Movies are also part of the store providing you with the option to purchase or rent a movie on any Apple device. iOS is also considered the most secure operating system on smartphones, as no viruses or malware can attack the smartphone making it the ultimate device for those that are always targeted by nasty software. You might wonder how this is possible as so many people are always complaining about viruses, well let me enlighten you. iOS is built upon a system called UNIX, which is considered the strongest, safest system to date. Therefore by building this into a smartphone gives you piece of mind. iOS is secure as it, for many other reasons that scare off some users, controls much of your experience with many "rules" to using this device. Many of these "rules" will not be affecting you directly as this might be your first smartphone. Existing smartphone users do not like the fact that you have to follow Apple's rules, such as not being able to share files to other smartphones (like Samsung or Nokia). iPhone does not allow expansion of the built in memory, where as other smartphones allow you to add a memory card for more storage of files. I personally feel that these features caters for another market of users and thus I encourage to educate yourself using my tools I give you to better understand what will work for you. I also feel that these rules allow me as a user to enjoy a safe smartphone I am comfortable storing personal information on.

Apple is very good at making sure that every user is able to share the same experience meaning that even after two or three years of owning an iPhone, you are able to enjoy the same operating system the newer iPhones are using. iOS can be automatically updated over-the-air, which means you don't need to plug it into a PC or Mac to update. iOS users will always have the option to upgrade for free to the latest offering from Apple.

iOS is a refined operating system with many features you will grow to love using. There is a really good balance of apps so that it would be almost impossible to be bored yet at the same time not overbearing with so many features that you are not sure where to start. iOS is easy to learn, though time spent with someone experienced will help you a bit more. Having the best application catalogue means that you will have all the apps available at your fingertips.

iOS will not disappoint and neither will the iPhone or iPad. I will recommend two smartphones and two tablets that Apple sells.

iPhone 5C

Apple have always catered to a very specific market, being the top level income market who love premium products with big price tags. That is Apple's approach and I would say it has worked out pretty well for them. Apple was routinely questioned when it will bring a lower cost iPhone as the market is starting to saturate and a low cost smartphone from Apple would be the answer. Apple released the iPhone 5C alongside the iPhone 5S and most did not get what they imagined Apple would show off. The public expected a very cheap iPhone but business as usual the iPhone 5C came out with a high price tag yet not failing to live up to that price with amazing features that you would normally find on an iPhone.

I personally really like the design of iPhone 5C, sporting a polyurethane encasing with 5 (Red, Green, Yellow, Blue and White) funky colours. The case itself is very durable, making it very attractive to new users that are scared they might smash it to pieces on the first day. The colours will suit any personality and is more a personal statement than anything else. Battery life will be enough to keep you going the whole day, perfect for those who might need to use it frequently. Camera quality will be more than enough for those starting out with a smartphone who enjoy taking photos. iPhone 5C will impress any user that is in the market for smartphone. Apple never intended for below par smartphones therefore you will not be disappointed as a budding smartphone user.

I would recommend this smartphone to anyone that is starting out, wants an up to date device and is willing to take some time to learn how to use the device. Experienced users might not be all impressed with this smartphone as it does not come with the latest hardware features. The iPhone 5C in essence is an iPhone 5 with a new physical design. I would say that the price tag might give some of you a scare so look around for the best price amongst carriers to ensure most value for money.

iPhone 5S

Best smartphone with highest customer satisfaction for five years can only sound impressive. iPhone 5S is Apple's main contender against the onslaught of smartphones that pop up every day and it is holding ground with all its might. iPhone 5S features a sleek design many try to imitate and it feels great in your hand while using. Aluminium encasing will mean lighter and thinner than most smartphones so this is really more a fashion statement too. Screen size is one of the most talked about topics regarding the iPhone. Apple says that the screen size is the perfect size to fit any hand, increasing the screen size will sacrifice many things that make this display so crystal clear. iPhone 5S screen is Retina Display, which means that the screen quality is beyond what your naked eye could distinguish. Retina Display is claimed to be past the quality your eyes can see, meaning if they would to improve it you will not be able to see the difference. You would need to follow my advice from the previous chapter to go experience the smartphone I recommend to really test out everything I am writing about. 8 megapixel camera with the slow-motion feature will attract many users. Apple is taking a road less travelled as that is not a double digit megapixel count like 95% of the smartphones. iPhone has a dual flash that allows more realistic looking photos. When using the flash while the large aperture, how much light the camera captures when taking the photo, will make it all that more lifelike. iPhone 5S also took a big step forward in terms of smartphone security with their user friendly fingerprint scanner that works most of the time. This feature allows you to unlock your iPhone with in an instant using your fingerprint, you are also able to purchase music and apps using this same method. It is close to flawless and this is purely the Apple style of doing things. Taking an early developed technology and refining it to the level that any user is able to enjoy the feature. Amazing camera capabilities, solid security and inspiring design makes this a very popular smartphone that many users will desire to experience.

I would recommend this smartphone to any level of user experience, any age, any person. This is my preferred choice of smartphones and I have been using iPhone since 2010.

iPad Mini Retina and iPad Air:

I will be talking about both of Apple's tablets that they are so similar that the only difference is the screen size.

iPad has changed the world and not a single person saw this coming. Remember how many laptops were carried around in the last couple of years? Can you see the difference? This is the result of the introduction of the iPad. We are now moving towards an era known as the post-PC era. Post-PC means that we are no longer so dependent on our laptops to perform daily tasks and we are moving towards an even more mobile age at a very fast pace. iPad is changing the face of school, business, entertainment and so many more industries and for a simple reason, being utterly and 100% mobile. iPad runs iOS, the same software as the iPhone but with a more "blown up" interface. If you would look at the same app on an iPad versus an iPhone you would not see a massive difference. The same elements will be on both apps with a difference format to suit the respective screen.

iPad will completely change the way you go about daily activities. Need to plan the kids schedule for the week? Enjoy a great 9.7" display to tap and swipe. Need to email and stay in touch with others? Massive on screen keyboard to type with more comfort than an iPhone. Want to read your favourite book? Enjoy Retina Display reading that will be an absolute treat to your eyes as the text looks sharp and clear. Need to use the iPad for the whole day? Enjoy a solid 10 hours if not more of battery life, some users I know charge their iPad once a week!

iPad's design is sleek and as attractive as an iPhone. You have the option of two screen sizes though the outside is the same. You will enjoy the extremely fast processor that will keep up with you!

5 megapixel camera will allow you to take standard quality photos, though I will not recommend this tablet for taking photos with a professional intent. It is advised to use the iPad for image processing after taken with another device as the Retina Display will give you 100% accurate colours and image contrast.

I say the iPad is the future of mobile communication, because the iPad caused major disruption in the desktop and laptop world as sales for PC's have been declining for 5 years and counting. iPads are replacing laptops and desktops left right and center. It is time to get on this band wagon and enjoy the ride into the future.

Do you really need a smartphone and tablet? Some say NO, others like myself say YES. iPhone and iPad makes a great combo if you know how to use it. You will do different tasks and intensity of work between iPhone and iPad.

iPhone will be used for most of your instant communication needs such as WhatsApp. You will take daily photo's with the iPhone as it sports a much better camera with more advanced features than iPad. You will also use iPhone for the most obvious reason; cellular calls. iPad will be used for tasks that require more screen space and thus boosting productivity as you are able to type faster, see more of the web page or read a book. The screen size on the iPad is what makes it the marvel it is. Movies and photos look amazing on the Retina Display.

I will recommend this tablet to anyone looking to slim down from a laptop, anyone that is looking for a tablet and anyone with any level of experience. I know some 70 year olds that are using iPad's to stay in touch with family and friends. Bingo and Bridge are the first apps to be installed for them as well as reading books. I would say more training is required using this device but there are places that will train you. There really is no other tablet I would recommend and the market share says the same. iPad's are accountable for more than 70% of the tablet market. Anyone can learn how to use this, it is truly the tool of the future.

Chapter 5

Juicy Berries

Blackberry was the standard for any businessman till today and is used by many South Africans. We all have grown to love checking our Blackberry's for the latest news on our friends, this was our first taste of true mobile social networking!

Brief History of Blackberry

Blackberry Limited, formerly known as Research In Motion(RIM) was founded by Mike Lazaridis and Doug Fregin in 1984 with wireless products in mind.

1988 - Shortly after their launch they became the first wireless data network in North America and started developing connectivity products for a company called MobiTex.

1992 - RIM developed a wireless point-of-sale device.

1996 - Their first true realisation of their vision was the release of a two way pager called the Inter@ctive Pager. This is what they wanted to bring to the world, wireless communication.

1998 - They release their latest version of a two way pager called RIM 950 Wireless Handheld. Their main product release this year was BlackBerry Enterprise Server which allowed e-mails to be sent and received securely on a mobile device. This was a massive breakthrough and the first glimpse of where we are today with wireless communications. We were able to stay in touch with clients no matter where we are. This was the start of the post PC era as people were no longer tied down to their desktop PC at the office.

2002 - BlackBerry launches their official first edition of a voice and data smartphone. The BlackBerry 5810! BlackBerry Enterprise Server also extends beyond the simple use of corporate e-mail but also corporate data and applications.

2004 - BlackBerry announces another major feature used still today, SureType. This year is also the start of Blackberry's reign in South Africa with the announcement to launch on MTN and Vodacom.

2005 - BlackBerry Enterprise Server receives FIPS 140-2 security certification. This is also another major breakthrough for mobile devices. This is BlackBerry's bread and butter, government approved security standard. Blackberry was the device for any government employee in USA.

2006 - Blackberry releases their first consumer-friendly smartphone, the Pearl edition range.

2007 - BlackBerry releases their well-known Curve range however Blackberry was unsuspectedly caught flat foot with the release of the iPhone.

2009 - App World is Blackberry's answer to the growing popular App Store by Apple.

2010 - Blackberry showcases their new operating system that will also power their early announced tablet to be released the next year.

2011, Blackberry releases the unpolished Playbook. It did not receive great reviews and very disappointing sales raised concern over the future of Blackberry. To top the year off, Blackberry Enterprise Service goes down for four days causing massive backlash from the public. This causes shares to drop drastically. Growing market share of other smartphones, such as Apple iPhone and Samsung, causes even more worry. South Africa however is the opposite for Blackberry. Unprecedented success here in South Africa grew bigger and bigger as twenty four month smartphone contract prices for these devices allowed consumers from every level of income to enjoy unlimited internet access.

2012 - Mike Lazaridis and Jim Basisle step down as co-CEOs. Stock is at all-time low of $6 per share.

2013 - The Q and Z range of Blackberry smartphones are announced, targeting specifically at the higher income consumer with advanced smartphone features and updated interface for their operating system. To date they have not been extremely popular as the Curve range was. Blackberry announces they are considering other alternatives for the company, including a sell off.

2014 - Blackberry releases extremely popular Blackberry Messenger to iOS and Android operating systems. Updated iterations of the Q and Z range is still struggling to gain traction. Blackberry announced dead in USA market as iOS and Android owns more than 85% of the smartphone market.

In South Africa, Blackberry has the biggest slice of the market share. Curve devices are very popular and cater for mostly the lower income market of South Africa. It is affordable and gives you access to the most sought after features of most smartphones today. R59 per month for unlimited internet access was a massive success as 3G data was very expensive. We all could keep in touch with Blackberry Messenger or also more commonly known as BBM. People were posting their BBM PIN online to connect to an even broader audience. No one used SMS, as BBM was the set standard for every level of consumer in South Africa. Teens, students, parents, teachers, service industries, adults and business men all loved the design, look and feel of a Blackberry Curve or Bold.

The QWERTY keyboard played another role in this success. The faster you could type a message the more popular you would be. This was the mentality of teens. Message broadcasting was another tool used to spread information around effectively. This was really the innovating technology that mesmerised the consumer market in South Africa. Blackberry was so successful in South Africa that in their last two to three years they have released every new smartphone here first in South Africa before other countries like USA and UK. Blackberry really made their mark in this country and it will still be just as popular in coming years in South Africa.

In the USA and the UK the Blackberry market is nothing if anything. Their delayed action of innovation against other brands such as Apple and Samsung, lead to their dropped market share around the world. Blackberry is still the standard for governments but there is no growing profit in those sectors. Consumer market equals profit and this is where Blackberry is struggling to get back. I personally do not believe they will ever be able to recover. I also don't believe they will shut their doors soon either. Their only hopes now are precious patents, social and security services and their smartphone line up. They are now focusing on Blackberry Messenger on other platforms, focusing on their intellectual property for their patents. They have always been about wireless, secure networking and they will hold onto that to the grave. They gave other smartphones too much of a chance to improve and refine their products that now they have to follow the standard. Blackberry will not just die as there are still millions of users relying on their services. They still produce a well-designed phone despite having lost their shine to the public.

I will now showcase the advantages and disadvantages of Blackberry's current lineup of smartphones. I will talk about the Q5 and Z30. These smartphones run on Blackberry 10, their latest operating system.

Blackberry 10

Blackberry 10 focuses on all the latest technology available to smartphones to assist with multitasking and staying connected to everything. This is the very clever mix of business and personal. New features were introduced such as Blackberry Hub, which is a convenient central hub for all your notifications such as e-mail, Facebook, BBM and calendar entries. ScreenShare allows other users to watch what you are doing on your smartphone screen.

This operating system relies heavily on swipes and gestures, this might prove challenging to you if you have never used a touch screen. My reasoning for this is that because navigating this smartphone requires time to learn how to do this. You might not remember all of them so I recommend this smartphone only to more experienced users. There is no document editor on this operating system, which might be a big set off if you need to have access to those tools.

I will recommend 2 devices and I will share my advice over each smartphone and from this I hope you will be able to make a decision if this smartphone will suit your needs. Remember that one of my bonuses included within this purchase is personal advice from myself on your next purchase of a device.

Blackberry Q5:

It is an entry level smartphone with great features most users will enjoy. Inexpensive for us and overall a good smartphone for someone that likes to stay in touch with personal and business contacts. The QWERTY keyboard makes this the ultimate type experience on smartphones. Touchscreen with physical keyboard makes a good combination but I would not suggest this to early smartphone users as this might prove challenging using two methods to navigate. Really great battery life, highly recommendable to business minded individuals and up to 12 hours of talk time.

Blackberry Z30:

This is the main smartphone that Blackberry presented to the public. With a massive touch screen with extensive battery life. This phone does not feel slow and seasoned Blackberry users will welcome this fresh updated approach to smartphones. No physical buttons makes it almost the opposite to what made Blackberry so successful, although the on screen keyboard is very well designed to give you similar speeds of typing. The only criticism I pass over this smartphone is that the user interface relies heavily on swipes, taps and gestures to navigate. Even I struggled the first hour with this smartphone to become reasonably comfortable. It is different to what others are doing and I guess this is good for Blackberry. I will only recommend this to users who are up for a challenge to something brand new. Great physical design makes it pleasing to the eye. All around a good smartphone that requires another year of refining before 100% ready for any type of user to utilize its' functions.

Blackberry is losing traction among smartphone users. I personally do not believe they make inferior products. They have just lost their market share to other brands because they only recently made an entry to the smartphone race. I would only recommend them to seasoned smartphone users in general.

New adopters of smartphones will struggle to understand what they tried to envision for a smartphone and will become frustrated with their purchase very easily. No one is 100% sure where Blackberry will go next, only time will tell.

Chapter 6

Tasty Desserts

Android has taken over the smartphone world in terms of market share. There are more than four million new devices activated each day on this platform. There is no doubt that Android has made their mark on smartphone development and should be considered a serious contender for the best smartphone you can own. Android is used by many big names including Samsung, Sony, HTC and very recently, even by Nokia. Android is open source, which means that it is free and manipulation is allowed by anyone who would like to add their own features to the smartphone.

So let me give you an example. Samsung got the Android operating systems altered so that the user interface was to their liking and therefore, put that software in their devices. They do not pay Google for anything and this is a very attractive option to consider if you do not have a solid in house operating system designed that you can install on your smartphones. Samsung has become ever more successful with their Galaxy series and considered the only match to the iPhone from Apple. I will talk about the massive difference between iOS, Apple's operating system, and Android as well as what it means for you when you purchase a smartphone or tablet.

Brief history of Android

2003 - Android Inc is born in Palo Alto, California. Andy Robin, Rich Miner, Chris White and Nick Sears work to develop an advanced operating system for camera. They soon found out that the market is not as big as anticipated thus they refocused their might and power to smartphone systems. They almost went bankrupt the same year before a generous donation was given to Andy Rubin who refused stakes in the company.

2005 - Android Inc is bought by Google Inc. Everyone thought that Google was going to enter the smartphone market. Patents revealed later that Google Inc would indeed do exactly. Final development of the Android operating systems allowed deals to be struck with hardware and cellular companies to allow the manufacture and sale of this new operating system on smartphones.

2007 - Android is caught by surprise, as Apple Inc releases a smartphone with a complete operating system. Their product was a mimic of a Blackberry design with QWERTY keyboard and no touch screen. Their entire focus shifted from physical to touch interface and later that year revealed an open source operating system that could be seen as a standard for smartphones. Many big name companies attended and supported Google with this standard set out.

2008 - Android version 1.0 is released on a smartphone from HTC dubbed HTC Dream.

2009 - Android version 1.5, named Cupcake, was released with an array of new features but it was not long till the next Android version 1.6, named Donut, was released. If that is not enough they released their last version for the year, being Android version 2.0, named Eclair.

2010 - Android version 2.2 named Froyo, short for Frozen Yogurt, is released on Googles release of the Nexus smartphone range that ran pure Android software, while partner companies designed the physical hardware. The Nexus range was seen as the top Android smartphone and set a standard for others to follow. Android version 2.3, named Gingerbread, was also released late this year.

2011 - Android version 3.0, named Honeycomb, was released and this was their first attempt at the tablet experience from growing competition of the Apple iPad. Android version 4, named Ice Cream Sandwich, was released and this was considered one of the first true polished versions of Android.

2012 - Android version 4.1, named Jelly Bean, was released with the aim to improve user experience in terms of smoothness and performance. Google releases their first tablet, Nexus 7 which was the first device to be shipped with Jelly Bean. Android is the most popular operating system in the world with the most installed user base overtaking Nokia and other vendors in shipments per quarter.

2013 - Android 4.4, named KitKat, was released. Many anticipated that version 5.0 would be released but this is kept for later.

Android went from almost bankrupt to the most used operating system in the world. Open source was their key to success, very much like Window's system in the 80's and 90's, as any vendor could install the software on their choice of hardware. This brought development costs down drastically although the responsibility was big with this business model. Why? Every single device you installed Android on had to be managed separately and many vendors stopped supporting newer features Android had to offer. Let me explain this is much greater detail:

Google makes the core software of Android. They make a blueprint of a smartphone operating system which then makes it free for anyone to download, tweak and ship for free. Let us use the example of Samsung as they are Android kings. Samsung designs their physical look and feel of a smartphone and they choose which hardware will be kitted to this smartphone. Samsung then modifies the Android core software to brand it to their choice, adding features their users demand. So now they are sitting with a unique looking operating system that will be installed on all their new devices.

If you followed closely on the history of Android you will notice there were many updates. Up to 3 per year! This creates a massive problem for Samsung. They need then to tweak the new Android operating system to look and feel like their brand. They do not update the software for all their previous models, as every single devices software needs to be updated. They do not see that as a viable option and simply stop supporting older devices. Their users now sit with an outdated version of Android. Not only is this very dangerous but it is also very disappointing and costly to us as we need to purchase a newer device to gain access to the latest offerings Android brings.

The dangerous part is that with every new Android release, security bugs or glitches are fixed to protect the user. Imagine you are sitting with a 2 year old device running old software that has a security bug that was fixed in an updated version, your smartphone with all of its personal sensitive information is open for attack. These attacks range from personal data stolen, devices wiped and cleaned from all information. The attacks would act as a virus on a desktop and there is nothing you can do as your software is not up to date. You can install anti-virus on your Android but it simply will not be enough, this is the major problem with Android and the vendors that use them for their smartphones and devices. There is no update all option for vendors and thus it does not make business sense to update older products as no profit gain will result in this practise.

The geeks will say this is no problem as they will simply force upgrade the smartphone using special techniques, but the majority of smartphone users are not geeks so this is not a viable option for you. You want a phone that will always have the latest features without you doing any major manual labor to attain it, unless you have excess money and do not mind buying a newer smartphone that supports the new Android software every couple of months. The majority of us that buy smartphones gets it with a two year contract with one of our cellular providers, therefore we have to very sure about the choice we make. I would like to take the opportunity again to promote one of the three bonuses of this book. I will personally advise you on which smartphone will work best for you.

Android is very popular for one simple reason, it's free. Free is good for most aspects but sometimes it causes more harm. Android is installed on the manufacturer's hardware. What this means to us is that the integration between these two components will never be 100%. Google makes the software and other companies make the hardware, they rarely work together to make the integration 100% such as the Nexus line up.

I would recommend Android to users that want to have the full on smartphone experience. You cannot go wrong with Android based smartphones. The great thing about Android is there are endless choices to choose from so there is definitely something for everyone. Android smartphones will range from size, price and overall performance and I will try and cover the essential Android smartphones to choose from.

I will now recommend devices from each of the mayor Android based smartphones in hope that you will be able to make an easy decision on which will work for you.

Sony Xperia Z2

Sony unveiled this smartphone very recently and it is not even available at the moment to the public. Why am I then advising you to take this smartphone? It has a camera that will blow you away, with the capability to shoot video in 4K quality. Now let me talk about 4K first. 4K is roughly three times better quality compared to standard full high definition quality. 4K video shooting capabilities will allow you to record all those meaningful moment in gorgeous quality that will almost seem unreal. I would recommend this smartphone for the photograph enthusiasts that do not always want to carry a heavy SLR camera with them. This will suffice for most photos in everyday life.

This smartphone has another trick up its sleeve. It is dust proof and waterproof. This is an issue that many users experience as we are always carrying our smartphone with us and how many times have we had an accident in the water or an outdoor trip turns out costly from dirt. This smartphone packs loads of punch with beefy specifications built on the inside. Hardware outpaced that most of us won't ever use but always nice to have. Sony has modified Android to their unique look and feel so you will have a different experience compared to other smartphones. Sony's skin over Android is very simple and easy to use and the big screen is bliss to those struggling to see what is displayed, although there are many features you will probably never use. I would recommend this smartphone primarily to users that like to have the latest smartphone features and even more refined to users that love their photographs and videos.

HTC One M8

HTC One M8 is HTC's second iteration of the so-called best Android smartphone to date, and they have done it again. HTC One M8 is named king of Android smartphones and for a very good reason. HTC was the first smartphone company to release Android, thus they have immense knowledge and experience that can be seen and felt with this premium designed smartphone experience. HTC, has taken the core Android software and modified it to their vision of the ultimate smartphone experience. HTC One has a huge display but it is still manageable, it will not overwhelm you like some smartphones. The encasing of this smartphone is metal, hence the "M" in its name, meaning it looks really good while protecting it from everyday activities. One thing that is very different to other smartphones is that the camera does not sport a two digit megapixel count, but rather a mere 4 megapixel.

If you read later on you will read about a smartphone that can take a whopping 41 megapixel photo. How does the best Android smartphone get away with a mere 4 megapixel? They work similar to Apple's approach to photo taking where the amount of megapixels mean nothing if the camera software behind it is not clever enough to use what is at its disposal. HTC reckons, it has been proven, that their technology behind their camera allows bigger pixels to be captured with each photo, more light is also captured, producing a more realistic photo than most 13 megapixel and above smartphone cameras. I have always liked HTC smartphones for their premium design and solid software that any experience level user will enjoy.

I would recommend this smartphone to any user. There is no specific niche user that this smartphone is aimed and I really understand why this smartphone is dubbed king of Android.

Nokia X, X+ and XL

The reason why I am doing something different with the Nokia X range is because they are so similarly priced that you can look at them as a whole. Going from the top to the bottom will not result in a significant price difference. The X range is Nokia's first attempt at Android on their hardware. Their main focus was providing you with great features for a really low price tag. These smartphones will be released with budget in mind so you pay what you get for. Nokia X is not available in South Africa at the time of publish, yet it was launched immediately in emerging countries around the world. News speculates it will arrive in South Africa soon. Nonetheless, Nokia X range is one of the easier to learn and this is yet again another major suggestion for someone switching from cellphone to smartphone. Not in the market for the best features but would like to be part of the smartphone revolution. All three smartphones come with large displays, the

XL, top of this range, has the largest. Camera is lower than standard, starts at 3 megapixel and top is 5 megapixel. Dual SIM card is another feature that makes this smartphone attractive to emerging markets.

When it becomes available I would highly recommend this smartphone to anyone that is just starting out with a tight budget in mind yet wants to enjoy the smartphone trend.

Samsung Galaxy S5

The 5th edition of the Samsung Galaxy S range is considered the best smartphone on the market at the moment, I too vouch for this. Samsung is leading the race with smartphone market share and there is no sign of slowing down either. Samsung has choke hold in terms of most smartphones shipped, surpassing Nokia. Samsung caters for every single level of income, as it has some very basic cheap cellphones and will have better versions right to the top with Galaxy S5. Samsung has altered Android core software and numbers to prove that there this is nothing short from top quality. Samsung, with Android, has 2 versions of their software. A basic and advanced mode, making it very attractive to any level of experience user. The basic version will be an extremely basic version of Android that will attract many users that want to switch to a smartphone. The advanced version is the main software, featuring countless tricks that will dazzle you at first but might wear off as the choice is too overwhelming to some.

Samsung focus heavily on internal upgrades of the hardware, which few would ever experience in its fullest might. I do however think that gamers and speed freaks would love this snappy smartphone that will always keep up with your tasks performed. Samsung Galaxy S5 is also waterproof and dust proof with a very high resistance. Keeping in mind that many new fitness features are included so outdoors are greatly suggested with this smartphone. Massive screen is one of the main reasons why it is so popular, the big colourful bright screen with easy to read text makes this smartphone a hit amongst those who prefer a bigger screen. New security features are in place to ensure safekeeping of your personal data to put your mind at ease. Fingerprint scanner to unlock your Samsung with options to pay using your fingerprint at certain vendors around the world, not available in South Africa. Samsung is pushing camera features to the edge with an impressive 0,3second focus time. This means no more blurry photos that you only notice after the action. This is truly a good contender for the mobile photographer enthusiast.

Fitness plays a major role in this Samsung smartphone as it updated its Fitness app that comes preinstalled. It will monitor vitals such as heart rate and calorie intake to promote a healthier you. Fitness is picking up traction and Samsung has released this with increasing marketing around the fitness features. Coupling the Galaxy Fit accessory with the Galaxy S5 makes a good attempt at comprehensive fitness and health monitoring, while not refined to the point that it would actually play a massive role on your decision to purchase this smartphone. Samsung Galaxy S5 adds another very new feature that most of you will love, Kids Mode. A safe environment your kids are allowed to access games without sending unexplainable emails to your colleagues or worse, your boss. Read the instruction manual before going into this mode or you might be stuck,

Samsung Galaxy S5 is one of few real contenders to the iPhone 5S. There is a great divide between the Samsung and Apple supporters. I feel both smartphones are worthwhile to consider yet the correct needs analysis is required to offer the right solution that you as the user would have the best experience with. I would recommend Samsung Galaxy S5 for those who want to experience the alternative to iPhone, someone that is new to smartphones and someone that isn't. This is a great smartphone and I am sure you will enjoy it. Retail stores in South Africa dedicated to Samsung products are opening up, allowing Samsung to further their grip on the smartphone industry.

Chapter 7

Funky Toppings

Nokia the former mobile device king! Every single person that is or will be using a smartphone started their journey with a Nokia, thanks Nokia. Nokia today is still part of the race even though they had a slow start with smartphones, merging with Windows to craft their vision of smartphones.

Brief History of Nokia

Nokia has one of the most interesting stories which very few know about. Nokia was started by a mining engineer, Fredrik Idestam, in the year 1865 as a wood pulp mill in Finland.

1871 - A second mill was opened at Nokianvirta river, which inspired the name Nokia.

1898 - Nokia joins up with another company to start the manufacturing of rubber.

1912 - Finnish Cable Works is another subsidiary of Nokia that become the foundation of their electronics business.

1960 - Finnish Cable Works produces their first electronic device, which was not a smartphone but a device used in nuclear power plants.

1963 - Focus turns to radio telephone development for government services. This was their first step into communications. They predicted and invested very early in telecommunications which paid off.

1981 - Nokia in conjunction with Salora launches world first international calling service.

1987 - Nokia releases their first edition of a true cellphone dubbed the Mobira Cityman with a price tag of about R67000. Global System for Mobile communication or more commonly known as GSM was also launched and Nokia was part of this development as they played a key role in this massively adopted technology ensuring Nokia's success for coming years.

1991 - The first GSM call was successfully made using Nokia technology.

1992 - Nokia releases their first digital GSM cellphone, the Nokia 1011. I am sure there are many of you that remember this iconic cellphone. This same year Nokia sold off all their other divisions to solely focus on cellphone technology.

1994 - Nokia releases the Nokia 2100 with over 20 million worldwide sales and their initial target for this cellphone was 400000 sales.

Talk about underestimation! This is the first time the legendary Nokia ringtone was installed on the cellphone. There is not a single person that does not know this cellphone ringtone.

1997 – Snake, the game, was installed and shipped with the Nokia cellphone. The original Angry Birds or Candy Crush that no one could get enough of. What was your high score?

1998 - Nokia is announced as the biggest cellphone manufacturer in the world.

1999 - Nokia releases their first web browser enabled cellphone with e-mail capabilities.

2001 - The first camera cellphone is released by none other than Nokia.

2002 - Nokia releases their first 3G enabled cellphone. Now cellphones could do what most smartphones focus on today. E-mail, browse the web, download music and watch videos online.

2011 - Nokia and Windows merge to reevaluate their approach to smartphones as they felt the heat from Apple and Samsung. Nokia Lumia smartphones are announced, which started their new line up of devices. Nokia Asha remains the top selling entry level cellphone in all developing counties.

Nokia was the cellphone powerhouse and not a single shred of doubt was in mind until Apple surprised everyone with their iPhone. Just like Blackberry, Nokia lost their massive hold on the market and today still struggle to find feet in the ever popular Apple and Samsung presence. Nokia did not foresee the overwhelming success from rivals that caused major disruption in their business model. Nokia was desperate and looked for assistance and Microsoft wilfully joined up with Nokia to take their shot at the new preferred way of cellphone technology.

Now today Nokia is relying heavily on their Microsoft Windows Mobile operating software. I believe the Nokia Lumia smartphone are one of the easiest to use on the market. This was what set Nokia apart from every other cellphone company, the ease of use that allowed any person of any skill or experience to use and love Nokia cellphones. The menu system, still today is simple and straight forward with almost no confusion. Nokia is also known for their superior build quality, great damage resistance and sleek design making it desirable.

Nokia is the only smartphone company that does not fully rely on Android to run their operating system, they use Windows Mobile. I loved this design from day one and always find it tempting to jump ship to this smartphone however for my own personal reasons I am sticking to my personal smartphone. Windows Mobile is all about a simple gorgeous interface on solid hardware that you will like instantly.

Windows Phone 8:

Windows Phone 8 is the latest offering from Microsoft. It has had a welcoming response as a brand new approach to smartphone operating systems. I myself really enjoy working on this smartphone, as it is very well laid out and navigating is a breeze. It features a tile style format where you tap on an icon and it will "flip" open to that application. It's very easy to learn. Live tiles allow a constant stream of information to display and update live on the screen, which is a very handy feature for anyone. All major smartphone features are included in this iteration of an operating system. You can easily connect via social network to upload content and share to the world with top quality camera hardware. Office for Windows Phone comes for free on all Windows Phone 8 smartphones. This is great news for us that need to use these tools everyday even if it means we are out of the office. I personally recommend this smartphone experience because I understood the operating system immediately and it is very simple to start using. I have also experienced something that will set back experienced smartphone users through the lack of app selection on the Windows Phone Store. Windows Phone 8 has received much criticism from users for their narrow selection of apps available. To make things worse, apps do eventually arrive but usually only months after the initial release from rival brands such as Apple and Android. I have looked at the apps selection and I did discover many apps unavailable that I rely on each day.

I will recommend 2 devices, I will share my advice on each smartphone and from this I hope you will be able to make a decision if this smartphone will suit your needs. Remember that one of my bonuses included with this purchase is personal advice from me personally on your next purchase of a device[5].

Nokia Lumia 620:

The entry level Nokia with Window Mobile 8, is a great phone with a low price. This smartphone comes with performance that will impress any user, young and old. The responsiveness and

[5] Please visit www.applesberriesdesserts.co.za to gain access to this exclusive content.

ease of use makes this smartphone look and feel like a top brand smartphone. Having Office included on this smartphone attracts many business conscious users that needs 24/7 access to this set of tools. I would highly recommend this smartphone to someone that has never used a smartphone and is conscious about price at the same time. Nokia Lumia 620 is one of my top recommended smartphones for any of you that want to start their new journey with a smartphone. Nokia and Microsoft really focused on ease of use within their operating system, high standard hardware and catering for every single sector.

Nokia Lumia 1020

This is the top level smartphone standard, with massive display and incredible camera power at your disposal. This smartphone is for those that want the latest, greatest and best features a smartphone can pack. Photographers would also fall in love with this smartphone for its incredible camera capabilities, which is 41megapixel. 41 megapixels sounds impressive even if you are not sure why. I will explain. You are able to capture a broader image than most other smartphones and thus this enables you more material to zoom in on. Office preinstalled makes the choice even easier because the massive display also enables comprehensive Word, Excel and PowerPoint editing. The great build makes for easy handling of the smartphone in day to day activity

Chapter 8

Choose Wisely

Never before have we ever been so bombarded with choice. This is 2014, which means technology is evolving by the day and it is not making it any easier for you. You are almost in a way forced to upgrade to this smartphone trend or you are without communication to the world and puts even more pressure on you, thus you rely solely on those around you to take advice. Purchasing smartphone and tablet should be as easy as walking into the shop and pointing out the smartphone you want, or at least asking or sharing information while interacting with the sales consultant to reassure your guess of which is the right choice. Sales consultants know how to control a sales interaction very easily if their buyer is inexperienced. They can share any information to you and 99% of it you will accept without question. The suggested solution from the sales consultant will very rarely be motivated purely by your needs. I want to empower you with tools that will enable you to make a more informed decision and not a decision a sloppy sales consultant presented. I do not have mall attitude towards sales consultant, there are some really amazing sales consultants that truly care about your needs and would do a proper sales cycle to determine possible solutions for you as an individual. Very few will not let their customers fall to self-motivated desires to a specific smartphone such as commission. Sales consultants are there to provide a customer experience and I intend to teach you how to make up your own mind for a smartphone before daring an interaction with the great South African sales team.

First thing is first, after reading my book you are welcome to email me (please visit www.applesberriesdesserts.co.za) so that I can give you a preliminary assessment of which smartphone will work best for you. This is the third amazing bonus included within this purchase of my book and I cannot wait to converse with all of you. We will briefly exchange emails to establish needs and make a recommendation that suits your needs and wants with a smartphone. I highly recommend this service to all those new to this world of smartphones and tablets. You can go to my website to send me an email with your details.

The second step is now to educate yourself around the recommended solutions I suggested. I need you to fully comprehend this product you are about to spend thousands on or sign two year contract for. I will make the suggestions, you will then follow my second bonus included with this book and that is to go to the websites provided to read up about the smartphone or tablet. I will share with you my most reliable sources for any information ranging from latest technology news, reviews, updates and the controversial rumorr mill.

We have to become confident, informed and excited to use this technology marvel of the 21st century. Internet will assist you greatly with endless information from top reviewers to amateur reports and the most importantly, regular users like yourself. You are to get informed about this product, what app market it uses, is the design appealing you, how much technical support and training is available. Where would you purchase this device and how much will it cost. How would it promote your activities daily, how you would interact socially with the device and most importantly, does it impress you? I would also not rely on a single website source to make up your mind and totally understand the device. Many websites are biased therefore doing sufficient research will enable a good understanding of what the general consensus say about the device.

You are more than welcome to talk to friends and family about their experiences with their smartphone or tablet, I would suggest asking questions such as:

How long does the battery last?

Who helps you when you have a problem?

How much do/did you pay for this?

What quality photos does it take?

Are you satisfied with the device?

There are many other questions to be asked but these basic questions are relevant across all smartphones. What you have done now is solid research you only can use as supporting evidence but certainly not final decision making. You simply educated yourself, there is one last step before you will achieve everything I teach in this book.

You are now to visit your preferred shop for purchase and you are to approach a sales consultant with your newly armed knowledge. Enough to make any sales consultant sweat! I would advise to ask similar questions as above but now you would want to ask additional questions such as:

What is the monthly/once-off cost?

Will you set it up?

What warranty does it come with?

Make sure the sales consultant is to showcase the features of the smartphone or device to you with a live device. I would stress to play with the device and get your personal feel for the device. Is it responsive enough, how does the screen size affect you, does the camera impress you etc.

I want you to spend significant time with the device, making sure you understand what the device offers to you. You are after all going to sign a two year contract or spend some amount of once off cash to get this device. You need to be 100% comfortable with your purchase and if you follow all my advice and use my bonuses I am very confident to say you will make the right decision.

I will explain now for the remainder of the book which smartphones each brand produces and why it might work for you. I will in detail discuss all the distinguishable features of each brand, why it will make a difference in your life and why you might be better off not taking the specified brand?

I have done extensive research over and above my lifetime dedication and passion to technology, this is a comprehensive guide on all mayor smartphones and tablets to consider for your next purchase.

Chapter 9

What Is Your App?

There is an app for anything you can think of. Apps are the future of smartphones and thus play a vital role in the success of a smartphone. I will explain what apps are, how to get the right apps and managing those apps.

App is short for application. A program designed to perform a certain task with a visual interface. Your smartphone comes loaded with apps that will perform the basic tasks of a smartphone. This will include e-mail, browser, calendar, weather, navigation, media player and camera. Not all of you will like the pre-loaded apps and thus you will search the market place for alternative apps. You might also find apps for things you never could imagine and thus the market place for apps plays a really big role in the experience of a smartphone. Every smartphone brand I talk about in this book has its own app market place. Apple has App Store, Android has Android Market, Blackberry has App World and Windows Phone has Windows Phone Market. To date, the Apple App Store has always been ahead of the race with the most curated app store available. It is also considered the safest app store to download apps from.

Developers prefer launching apps on App Store from Apple as the adoption rate from users is immense compared to other market places. There is also more profit involved with launching apps on the App Store, as developers take 70% of profits from every app that is purchased on the App Store. Apps are available for all smartphones and I would say that app availability for a smartphone is everything, over and above other features. You will download apps for any and all things that will make the smartphone so great. Want to know what the latest ZAR to USD conversion is? There is an app for that for that. Want to book flights instantly? There is an app for that. Want to look at the sky and be able to say which star is which? There is an app for that.

I rely on apps everyday. I use apps to capture customer details, compare prices of products, share documents between colleagues, play games, edit photos and even manage my finances every month. Apps will range from informative to fun uses and thus this is why I state that apps make up everything about the smartphone you choose. Apps have super-fast access to whatever information you need at this very second, which usually we'd have to go on a website to get the information we need. Before smartphones we needed to actually wait to be on a desktop PC to access the information we so desperately needed at that moment in time. The major difference between an app and mobile website is that the website needs to be updated and refreshed every time you use it, where as an app also relies on this method but most of the data can be loaded with the app so not as much data is required to see the same information.

Here is an example to explain it clearly.

If you want to get the latest conversion rate of two currencies you would go to your browser on your smartphone, type the address in for the website, wait for the website to load, choose your currencies with the data and then press convert. If you had the app installed on your smartphone, you would simply tap on the icon on your screen, type in the conversion data and press convert. The time difference is almost ¾ times faster. Less data was used with the app in order to load the exact same results portrayed by both methods. I can use the same comparison when you want to look at the weather forecast. Opening an app versus going to your web browser and taking about three steps to perform the same task. Apps will differ between a smartphone and tablet. Apple is leading the race when it comes to tablet market share and market penetration of tablet. Thus this is very good news for you as the developers are designing apps specifically made for the iPad screen size. You will get a custom designed interface that will be a joy to work with even though you are using an iPad. The difference between a smartphone and tablet screen is that the app can be formatted to work more efficiently as there is more screen space available. Developers for App Store usually launch their apps on this market first where they sell many licenses and continue to improve the apps, most of the times for free. You can download the same app onto multiple devices and access them at any place in the house or office.

I would highly suggest to explore your installed app market on your smartphone and don't be scared to explore and see what is on offer. There are some really great apps designed for almost every purpose imagined. You will find a mix of paid and free apps but generally the free version is like a demo so you can test run the app before you invest in this app. I have made countless purchases on great apps I use everyday, I spend most of my money on games actually. App markets are vast and at times you might not always know that there is an app for something specific that you might want to do, therefore you can see what the app market has to offer on their featured pages, which will showcase the latest and greatest. I have included with this purchase a free copy of recommended apps for you to get that will get you started with your new smartphone. My other free bonus included with this book is a collection of great website you can read up in your own time to keep up to date with smartphone and tablet news. [6]

Apps that cost a fee to use, may be a once off or subscription payment and you will pay this via credit card. You will need to sign up for an account to make purchases and download free apps. This account will usually be one for everything on the smartphone so less passwords to remember for us. Apps also use a new model of releasing for free but when you need to get access to special features of the app you would need to pay. This allows variety of content to be made available to users that might be interested.

Apps might also go the route of subscription like recently launched Microsoft Office for iPad. The app is free to download but you need to pay a yearly subscription to actually use the app. You can view documents with the free version but you cannot create documents. Games use the model of free release but paid content for in-game currency. You can play the game as long as you want but if you want to purchase new clothes, skill up or move to new levels you need to pay with money to proceed. There has been much controversy of kids using their parents' device and run up a bill over R100000. Your credit card is linked to the account of the app market and especially with games, as I just explained, kids want to progress to new levels or purchase new

[6] Visit www.applesberriesdesserts.co.za for access to this content

items, which leads to their parents being charged for that. Apple has been very kind about this matter and has even offered to repay parents with ridiculous accounts run up by their kids.

The other side of this credit card linked to app market account is that there are thief's that steal those credentials through other manners and running up an account. People could have been negligent with safety of those details or let someone else use their accounts. The app market takes no responsibility with that therefore you have to be very careful in keep your credit card details safe. No app market has had a security break where our details have been exposed and used maliciously so I won't worry about that.

App markets are secure channels to browse and download new apps for your device. The problem might be that the app market is not actively curating the market and ensuring that apps submitted for download are safe and secure. App Store from Apple is doing an immensely great job at making sure that the bad apps stay out and that the apps are doing what the developer is advertising it will perform to you as a user. Apple inspects every single app before made available to the App Store. I feel strongly about this as I am extremely reliant on apps for the success of my daily activities and I expect any app, that is made available, to perform the task advertised and at the same time not use my personal data on my smartphone for other malicious uses. Many apps have been banned from app markets for extracting irrelevant information in order to work.

You might wonder what I am saying so let me explain. I download app "X" which states in their description that it will edit photos I choose with a wide variety of filters to make it look unique. I download the app as I have a need for a photo editing app. I use my account to make the purchase and the download starts. I open the app and it requests that in order for it to work, it needs access to my photos, contact number list as well as my microphone. Your smartphone should clearly ask you if you allow the app to access the specified data. I read the description before downloading the app and it simply stated it would edit my photos. So what on earth does it need to have access to my contact list and microphone? I have used countless photo edit apps and they only request for photo access. My best advice about this app to you? Report it to your app market place. This app was designed for reasons other than stated on the description and you should look at apps like products you would normally purchase at a shop. You read the description and you expect it to fully live out that description and if it doesn't we are very easily liberated to question the seller. This works the same when purchasing anything from app markets.

Also do not think this only happens with charged apps. Free apps could also be designed for underlying reasons not visible at first. It would advertise to perform certain tasks but when you open it, it does not even look the same as on the app market. This is a massive difference between Android and Apple. Apple inspects every single app submission to App Store, over 1 million apps are available to download today, and undergoes in-depth reviews before released on the App Store. Some reviews take up to weeks before the app will go live. Apple also enforces an extremely strict policy of no explicit adult apps on App Store, this is great for any parent that thinks of purchasing a tablet or smartphone for their youngsters.

Android Market unfortunately is not that strict when it comes to what goes on their market. There is some measurement of review of the apps that goes live but it is still very wild and free for anyone to post any kind of explicit adult content or malicious apps that use your data for the wrong reasons. These are the questions you need to ask before buying a smartphone and I will, mentioning the free bonuses again, give you a free mini app guide book and personal advice on which smartphone will work for you best.

In closing, apps are what make smartphones so special. New apps are being made daily and if there is not an app for your needs I am sure someone is already developing one for you.

Chapter 10

Staying Safe

Privacy[7] is one of the most talked about topics in this new era of technology. I will share my thoughts and advice about privacy and demonstrate why it is so vital to understand where we are with privacy. Remember I said technology is a blessing and a curse? Now I will talk a little bit about the curse side of technology and how it is used for the wrong reasons and how it affects your personal life.

We all use social networks to stay in touch with friends and family, to see what your favourite companies or brands are up to. We are using social media to stay up to date with our favourite celebs and to share news amongst each other. We use social networking to share important life events such as a newborn baby or getting married. We are using social networks to post the other new fad, selfies. Social media is great and I use it myself to stay in touch with the latest technology trends. I use it for checking what events are planned by my favourite musicians. I use social media to browse photos mostly in my interest. We are investing an awful lot of personal information on the social networks that certain questions are starting to come to mind that might unsettle some and others will simply write the idea off. Facebook started out as an inter university social network where students could post relevant updates, have a bio and be able to message other students instantly. Today they have over one billion users around

---

[7] Dictionary.com announced "privacy" Word of The Year 2013

the world. That escalated very quickly and I feel people are going to start asking relevant questions to this matter with great urgency. Do you know that any information, media or message that is sent on Facebook is the property of Facebook? They own the right to use, store and delete it at will?

Let's review my opening paragraph. Facebook knows who your friends and family are; who and what is your favourite brand and even know who your secret crush is. They know about every single important life event, the date and location of your newborn baby and how long you have been married or how long you have been single. They own every individual photo you upload, all those photos of your cats and awkward selfies. I remember when I was much younger and it was almost a crime to use your personal details on the internet. I would always hear these horrid stories about how people's identities were stolen. I was even almost afraid of the internet back then because it was not consumer friendly, it was mostly for the hackers and the computer geeks.

The internet was unsafe, unregulated and unprotected from malicious attacks. People would never have invested any kind of personal information. Today there are websites dedicated to posting your whole personal life for the world, or your friends at least, to see.

I am not saying that technology is evil and the lack of privacy is the end of human freedom. I am saying that you should watch what you post online for others to see. Know which apps are using what personal data to function. Understand that you do not own anything posted on social media. Understand that there are people who will use it to stalk or potentially harm you. We are living in the free-for-all internet world and anything goes.

Chapter 11

Update Complete

South Africa is one of the largest emerging market in terms of smartphones and tablets; we have simply tasted a small piece of the bigger picture of this amazing technology and I cannot wait to see where it will all go. Technology is the essence of evolution, it is meant to be and everyone will at some point in their lives interact and experience it. I am ready to embrace this modern age; I know you can be ready with me. My guidebook's intent was to show everyone an easy way to understand this shift we are undergoing.

Let's all work together to educate each other around the current affairs of smartphones and tablets and keep the information flowing. We have to keep up with the information age, we have to be connected.

Please visit www.applesberriesdesserts.co.za for more information.

;)

Appendix

Sources

- Sony Mobile. (2014). *Sony Xperia Z2.* Available: http://www.sonymobile.com/za/products/phones/xperia-z2/?utm_source=marketing-url&utm_medium=/za/products/phones/xperia-z2/&utm_campaign=http://www.sonymobile.com/xperia-z2. Last accessed 31 March 2014.

- Sony Mobile. (2014). *Sony Xperia Z2 Features.* Available: http://www.sonymobile.com/global-en/products/phones/xperia-z2/features/#Display. Last accessed 2014.

- Dan Grabham. (2014). *Sony Xperia Z2 release date, news and features.* Available: http://www.techradar.com/news/phone-and-communications/mobile-phones/sony-xperia-z2-release-date-news-and-rumors-1215763. Last accessed 31 March 2014.

- Tom Parson. (28 March 2014). *HTC One (M8) review.* Available: http://www.stuff.tv/htc/htc-one-2/review. Last accessed 31 March 2014.

- HTC. (2014). *HTC One (M8) Specs..* Available: http://www.htc.com/us/smartphones/htc-one-m8/. Last accessed 31 March 2014.

- Nokia. (2014). *Nokia X Dual SIM.* Available: http://www.nokia.com/global/products/phone/nokia-x/. Last accessed 31 March 2014.

- Gareth Beavis. (14 March 2014). *Hands on: Nokia X review.* Available: http://www.techradar.com/reviews/phones/mobile-phones/nokia-x-1227006/review. Last accessed 31 March 2014.

- http://www.samsung.com/global/microsite/galaxys5/features.html

- HTC. (2014). *UltraPixels and Sensor Size.* Available: http://www.htc.com/www/zoe/ultrapixel-sensor-size/. Last accessed 31 March 2014.

- Global News and The Canadian Press. (24 September 2013). *BlackBerry timeline: A look back at the tech company's history*. Available: http://globalnews.ca/news/860689/blackberry-timeline-a-look-back-at-the-tech-companys-history/. Last accessed 31 March 2014.
- Blackberry. (2014). *Blackberry Z30*. Available: http://za.blackberry.com/smartphones/blackberry-z30.html. Last accessed 31 March 2014.
- Blackberry. (2014). *Blackberry*. Available: http://za.blackberry.com/. Last accessed 31 March 2014.
- Nokia. (2014). *The Nokia story*. Available: http://www.nokia.com/global/about-nokia/about-us/the-nokia-story/. Last accessed 31 March 2014.
- Windows Phone. (2014). *Nokia Lumia 620*. Available: http://www.windowsphone.com/en-za/phones/nokia-lumia-620?model=rm-846. Last accessed 31 March 2014.

- Compuware. (2012). *What Consumers Really Need and Want*. Available: http://offers2.compuware.com/rs/compuware/images/Mobile_App_Survey_Report.pdf. Last accessed 31 March 2014.

- Wikipedia. (2014). *Android Version History*. Available: http://en.wikipedia.org/wiki/Android_version_history. Last accessed 31 March 2014.

Special Thanks

My dearest Mother that always believed in me, motivated me to go further and achieve whatever I set my mind to.

To Romi, thank you for the infinite love, patience and understanding for what I do.

Biggest thank you to Steven for all your support, I could not have done it without you.

A special thanks to Lauren for editing my book.

Big thanks for *aeronaughtycal* for superb web skills!   Warm thanks for *janielescueta* for the outstanding front- and back cover.[8]

Thanks Terence, Justine, Morne and Elmo for all the insightful knowledge, ideas, criticism and input towards this book.

Thank you Chaim for being the catalyst of this book, you are the most amazing person and I dedicate this book to you.

Last but not least, Raymond Aaron that believed in me and gave me the opportunity to write this book using his expertise and knowledge.

Anyone I did not mention:

THANK YOU FOR ANY CONTRIBUTION TO THIS BOOK!

---

[8] You can find these amazing artist on www.fiverr.com

www.ingramcontent.com/pod-product-compliance
Lightning Source LLC
Chambersburg PA
CBHW061027050326
40689CB00012B/2728